FOR CHILDREN WHO WERE BROKEN...
WRITTEN BY ELIA WISE

BERKLEY BOOKS, NEW YORK

This Berkley book contains the complete text
of the original edition. It has been
completely reset in a typeface designed for easy
reading and was printed from new film.

FOR CHILDREN WHO WERE BROKEN...

A Berkley Book / published by arrangement with the author

PRINTING HISTORY
Previously published by the author, 1989
Berkley trade paperback edition / October 1991

ISBN 0-425-12974-8

A BERKLEY BOOK® TM 757,375
Berkley Books are published by The Berkley Publishing Group,
200 Madison Avenue, New York, New York 10016.
The name "Berkley" and the "B" logo
are trademarks belonging to Berkley Publishing Corporation.

PRINTED IN THE UNITED STATES OF AMERICA

10 9 8 7 6 5 4 3 2 1

FOR CHILDREN WHO WERE BROKEN...

For children who were broken,
it is very hard to mend . . .

Our pain was rarely spoken
and we hid the truth from friends.

Our parents said they loved us,
but they didn't act that way.
They broke our hearts
and stole our worth,
with the things that they would say.

We wanted them to love us.
We didn't know what we did
to make them yell at us
and hit us,
and wish we weren't their kid.

They'd beat us up and scream at us
and blame us for their lives.
Then they'd hold us close inside their arms
and tell us confusing lies
of how they really loved us—
even though we were BAD,
and how it was OUR fault they hit us,
OUR fault that they were mad.

When days were just beginning
we sometimes prayed for them to end,
and when the pain kept coming,
we learned to just pretend
that we were good
and so were they
and this was just
one of those days...
tomorrow we'd be friends.

We had to believe it so.
We had nowhere else to go.

Each day that we pretended,
we replaced reality
with lies, or dreams,
or angry schemes,
in search of dignity . . .
until our lies
got bigger than the truth,
and we had no one real to be.

Our bodies were forsaken.
With no safe place to hide,
we learned to stop
hearing and feeling
what they did to our outsides.

We tried to make them love us,
till we hated ourselves instead,
and couldn't see a way out,
and wished that they were dead.
We scared ourselves by thinking that,
and scared ourselves to know,
that we were acting *just like them*—
and might evermore be so.

To be half the size of a grown-up
and trapped inside their pain ...
To every day lose everything
with no savior or refrain ...
To wonder how it's possible
that God could so forget
the worthy child you knew you were,
when you'd not been damaged yet ...
To figure on your fingers
that the years till you'd be grown
enough to leave the torment
and survive away from home,
were more than you could count to,
or more than you could bear,
was the reality we lived in
and we knew it wasn't fair.

We who grew up broken
are somewhat out of time,
struggling to mend our childhood,
when our peers are in their prime.
Where others find love
and contentment,
we still often have to strive
to remember we are worthy,
and heroes just to be alive.

Some of us are healing.

Some are stealing.

Most are passing the anger on.

Some give their lives away to drugs,

or the promise of life beyond.

Some still hide from society.

Some struggle to belong.

But all of us are wishing

the past would not hold on

so long.

There's a lot of digging down to do
to find the child within,
to love away the ugly pain
and feel innocence again.
There's forgiveness
worthy of angel's wings
for remembering those at all,
who abused our sacred childhood
and programmed us to fall.
To seek to understand them,
and how their pain became our own,
is to risk the ground we stand on
to climb the mountain home.

The journey is not so lonely
as in the past it's been . . .
More of us are strong enough
to let the growth begin.
But while we're trekking
up the mountain
we need everything we've got,
to face the adults we have become,
and all that we are not.

So when you see us weary
from the day's internal climb...
When we find fault
with your best efforts,
or treat imperfection
as purposeful crime...
When you see our quick defenses,
our efforts to control,
our readiness to form a plan
of unrealistic goals...
When we run into a conflict
and fight to the bitter end,
remember...
We think that winning means
we won't be hurt again.

When we abandon OUR thoughts
and feelings,
to be what we believe YOU
want us to,
or look at trouble we're having,
and want to blame it all on you...
When life calls for new beginnings,
and we fear they're doomed to end,
remember...
Wounded trust is like a wounded knee—
It's very hard to bend.

Please remember this
when we're out of sorts.
Tell us the truth, and be our friend.
For children who were broken...
it is very hard to mend.

*   *   *   END   *   *   *